Pieces of Priscilla

By Priscilla Johnson

Charlie's Port
FRINGE Imprint

Publisher's Note: This is an autobiographical work. Some names and places have been changed to protect the innocent. All ideas and information are the product of Priscilla Johnson's personal recollection of her life. Poetry was conceived in her imagination between the ages of 13 and 15. All illustrations were created by Priscilla Johnson.

Book design & Cover design © 2022 STUDIOCUDICIO

Special discounts are available on quantity purchases by corporations, associations, and others. For details, contact the publisher at
info@charliesport.org

Pieces of Priscilla / Priscilla Johnson
ISBN Print: 978-0-9997510-1-5

Printed in the United States of America for distribution in the U.S. / Canada / UK / Europe / Australia

Pieces of Priscilla

By Priscilla Johnson

TABLE OF CONTENTS

Prologue

I believe that, in a way, we are all searching for our Great Perhaps. You see, this Great Perhaps symbolizes something I, and most others, desperately want: answers. For me, writing is a way of searching. The poems in this book aren't just poems, but pieces of me. Into each one I've poured all the things that I have tried so hard to forget. I've poured into every poem just a little bit of the hurt, the pain, and the sadness that I've felt over the years. For me, writing started out as an escape; today, it's a necessity. I rely on pen and paper just as heavily as one might rely on air, water, and food. Through writing, I've learned that it's okay to feel, it's okay to hurt.

My name is Priscilla Johnson. What you are holding isn't just a book; it isn't just a story. These poems are an extension of me, and I'm entrusting them to you, so hold me carefully. My past is a sad and difficult place, but you won't be able to understand my poems unless you first understand me. The first step is understanding that when I talk about my family, I am never referring to my biological parents. Any relative that I talk about except my sister Marie, I mean the family that adopted me.

At the age of two, I was put into foster care. For five years I lived in home after home, with family after family. Two months before my eighth birthday, in May 2011, my twelfth foster family adopted me. Moving all your life, never having a mom or dad, a grandma or grandpa, would be enough to scar anyone. But it wasn't just the constant unsettlement that scarred me, it was the people.

> "The thing is, when you lose someone, you realize you'll eventually lose everyone."
>
> —John Green, Turtles All the Way Down

For a while after my first adoption, life was perfect. I had everything I wanted. Finally I had a family. But in fifth grade, my pap got sick. A couple months later, he died of cancer.

In sixth grade, I was bullied by my best friend. I naively believed she would come back to me, but she never did. I wanted to die. If I couldn't trust her, then whom could I trust? My world had been shattered into millions of tiny fragments. I wanted to let go.

About halfway through sixth grade I found out we were leaving Pennsylvania. I can't begin to explain how angry and upset I was. I guess you could say I was passionately enraged. I hated change of any kind, and still do. Although my hatred has subsided over the years, even the tiniest changes used to upset me. For example, I used to hate it when my mom got a haircut because she always came back with a new style. It made her look different. I didn't like different. I've come a long way, though. At least I talk to her now after she gets a haircut.

When I was in foster care I was always moving. In some homes I stayed little more than a month. I never knew if I would wake up to find my suitcase packed. I never knew where I was going or how long I'd be staying.

That seventh-grade move was extremely hard for me. I would be seventeen hours away from everything familiar, everything I had ever known. When my parents and I viewed the condo that we'd eventually end up living in, I refused to even look at it. I sat on the floor, in front of everybody, and cried. I just wanted to go home. Eventually, I ended up loving it. I would never move back, not even if I had the choice. I have made better and truer friends than the ones I left behind. I can't imagine being anywhere else with anyone else.

I attended a church camp only two weeks after we moved. Despite how adamant I was to *not* make friends, I made some anyway. It was at camp that I realized how tired I was of being angry, how tired I was of being sad and bitter and depressed. I wanted to be happy again. Once I opened myself up to the possibility of happiness, I was able to do something that would change my life forever: I found Jesus. I came home not just happy, but overjoyed. I was no longer seeing everything in black and white. The world had color again.

That school year I made a few friends, but soon I was being bullied again. What's worse, those kids knew nothing about me. All they knew was that I was different and that my differentness threatened their state of normality. That same year, my grandfather almost died of heart failure. He couldn't be with us at Christmas. It was the first time I had spent Christmas without him since my adoption.

When I was in eighth grade, my father was diagnosed with prostate cancer. He went through treatments, and his cancer went into remission. But it was scary.

When I was in ninth grade, my mema got sick. After many hospital visits and a lot of overnight stays, we were delivered the ground-shaking news that she also had cancer. Non-Hodgkin's lymphoma, to be exact. Watching someone I loved suffer slowly and painfully broke me. She died just five months after she was diagnosed. For months after her death, I refused to believe she was gone. The world had, once again, begun to lose its color.

Yet, here I am, despite it all, still living.

> "In three words I can sum up everything I've learned about life: it goes on."
>
> —Robert Frost

Robert Frost is right. Life goes on. So must I. Through all that heartbreak, I made new friends, friends that changed me, shaped me, made me better. I love these friends with every atom in my body. They make me smile when I don't want to. They make me laugh when all I want to do is cry. When I hurt, they hurt with me. I no longer have to go through anything alone. When I'm down, they don't leave me to drown on my own. They pick me up and put me back on my feet. So, shout-out to you (you know who you are). Keep being you, you amazingly beautiful, adorable, huggable people.

I hope to make something of myself one day, to be an author, to help people, to inspire them. I want them to see the world not only as it is, but also as it could be. My wish for you, dear reader, is that you'll come upon the same realization. I hope you'll find as much comfort and solace in words as I do, and that you'll come to see books as more than just paper and ink. When you read these poems, I hope you *feel* them. I believe we are all searching for something that will give us answers. So, here's to all the Great Perhapses that have yet to be discovered.

Priscilla Johnson

Foster Care

"It's a paper town... All those paper people living in their paper houses, burning the future to stay warm."

—John Green, Paper Towns

LITTLE GIRL

Little girl,
lone girl,
all alone girl.
No one but her teddy bear.
Changing faces,
all new places.
Never knowing where she's going,
or where she will end up.
Hiding under the bed,
thoughts swirling around her head.
She won't go back.
She won't go with them.
She won't leave again.
She can't leave again.

This is the only place
she's ever known love.

I was in foster care for four and a half years. During those years, I lived in twelve different foster homes. Foster care was all I had ever known. I didn't know what "home" truly meant. *How was a mom supposed to act? How did love feel? What did a family look like?* I didn't know.

My biological parents were never really my parents and they never will be. Parents *choose* you and love you no matter what you have done. They're there for you when you need them, when you want them, and even when you don't. They were given a choice, and they didn't choose me; they didn't choose us.

They were, from what I understand, drug addicts, alcoholics, or (most likely) both. Time and again they were told that if they didn't get sober, if they didn't take care of their kids, somebody else would do it for them. We would be taken from them.

They would always beg and plead. "Don't take away our children!" they'd cry. "We'll stop, we'll get sober. We'll do whatever it takes. Just don't take our kids."

Spoiler alert: they didn't stop. They didn't get sober, and they didn't keep their kids. They were given chance after chance. No matter how many times they said they loved us, no matter how much they insisted that they cared, we were never their top priority. In the end, they chose drugs over all my brothers, my sister, and me. They chose alcohol over the children they made. They loved us, sure, just not enough to choose us. They knowingly brought children into this world, yet they did nothing to ensure our survival in it.

My sister's death was the last straw. My younger sister, who was about fourteen months at the time of the accident, somehow fell into the kiddy pool and drowned. My older brother jumped in and tried to save her, but he was too late. My father, upon seeing the lifeless body of his baby girl in the arms of his son, lost control. In his rage, he punched my brother. Someone, somewhere, amid all the confusion and chaos, called the police. My sister had been dead for ten minutes before they were able to revive her. Yes, they brought her back, but she hasn't been the same since.

My little sister wasn't born disabled. She was born with zero abnormalities, but because our parents couldn't commit to being there for their own children, my sister now has to live a life she didn't choose, one she didn't want. We were told that she would never walk on her own. She'd never talk, never be able to eat, bathe, do anything. She'd always be dependent on someone else to take care of her. She has defied all logic and now does every one of those things on her own. But she'll never be the same. The water damaged her brain. My sister is disabled, and it isn't her fault.

After her accident, my brothers and I were placed into a foster home. For me, it would be the first of twelve. I spent years moving around, bouncing from place to place. I never knew where I would be staying or how long I would be there. I had no say in anything.

One family told me they'd be my "forever family," yet the very same people told me, over and over again, that I would never be enough, that no one would ever adopt me. To them, I was a monster, unworthy of love. They told me I wasn't good enough to be their daughter, that I didn't deserve to be part of their family.

They would lock me in my room when I aggravated them. They'd bring me food when they had to. I have severe ADHD, and it was even worse for me back then. Keeping any normal kid locked up in their room for hours on end would be awful, but for me it was horrific. They gave me the guest room. It had zero decorations, zero toys. It wasn't kid friendly in any way. To put it plainly, it wasn't home.

I was only with them for about six months. As I was packing up to move, I got into an argument with my foster mother. I don't even remember what it was about. I remember her raising her hand to hit me, and I remember crumpling to the floor. I curled into the fetal position and waited. She hadn't hit me, but only because her husband had stopped her. She didn't care about the law, that it was illegal to hit a foster child. She insisted that I had to be taught a lesson. I cried. It is my first and only memory of pure fear. She yanked me off the floor and screamed at me, told me to finish packing. She was going to stand in the doorway and watch because I didn't deserve her help. At one point, I stubbed my toe on the foot of the bed. I looked to my foster mother, because no matter how awful she was to me, I still craved her love and affection. I told her I had hurt my toe.

She squatted down, looked me right in the eyes, and said, "That pain is God paying you back for everything you ever did to us."

I didn't understand. *What had I done?* Years after I left their home, her words still echoed in my brain. *How was I the monster?*

In foster care, I was never scared of the monsters in my closet, or the ones under my bed. I would have welcomed them any day. I was scared of the people I was being forced to live with.

I know now that I wasn't an easy child to foster. I had issues, but I was just a kid. I didn't understand that then. I had reactive attachment disorder, a rare but serious condition in which infants and young children don't establish healthy bonds with parents or caregivers. Those children are typically neglected, abused, or orphaned. RAD develops when the fundamental needs of comfort, affection, and nurturing are unmet. Thus loving, caring attachments with others are never established. This may permanently change the child's growing brain, impairing the ability to establish future relationships.

In my case, it was emotional neglect. My previous guardians and foster parents had failed, or even refused, to meet my emotional needs. Moving from home to home also limited my ability to form bonds and attachments. I've even been told that I didn't (for the most part) respond to physical pain. I was more social with complete strangers than I was with my own foster parents; I talked incessantly, was hyperactive, a chronic liar, hypervigilant, and extremely controlling. I had no sense of right and wrong, had horrible impulse control, and so on. (Hyperactivity and poor impulse control are also symptoms of my ADHD.) In short, I wasn't connected to reality. I wasn't really there.

Foster care scarred me, mentally and emotionally. I never had the childhood every kid dreams of. It hurts, even now, to think of that home. *Why would an adult tell a child God is punishing her?* It hurts to think about how my parents didn't want me, how they couldn't choose me. It angers me to think about what they did to my little sister. Foster care, seen through the eyes of a foster parent, is sad and hard. Seen through the eyes of the foster child, it is devastating. I'll never get those four and a half years back. I was in the system from the age of two till the age of eight.

I still have memories of my biological parents. I want to think of them as good people, caring and loving people, but I can't. Nothing can change the fact that they practically abandoned us. Nothing can change the fact that they didn't choose me.

But I've been adopted for almost nine years now. I have a family that did choose me, that does love and care about me. No matter how much I disappoint them, they don't give up on me. The people that gave birth to me aren't my parents and they never will be. My parents are the people that chose me, and I wouldn't trade them for the world.

TELL HER WHY

Look her in the eyes
and tell her,
tell her why she has to move again.
Tell her why no one came to say goodbye.
Tell her that she has issues.
Explain why no one wants her.
Tell her it's completely implausible
she'll ever be adopted.
Go ahead and crush her dreams under your foot.
Go ahead and tell her
how utterly demonic she is.
Tell the six-year-old
that she'll never be loved,
but don't forget to tell her that it's
not her fault.

It's not her fault,
she didn't choose her scars.
She didn't choose this life.
She didn't choose to be treated
like a pair of hand-me-down shorts.
She doesn't want your insults,
she's already scared.
Not of the monsters in her closet
but of the humans that she lives with.

MY BROKEN LITTLE HEART

It was always me, myself, and I
and the crackling static in my ears,
along with those distant, blurry figures
who seemed almost to float.
Their blinding smiles
and outstretched arms
gave a false sense of security to
my lonely little heart.

I pushed them away,
afraid to feel,
afraid of love,
of rejection,
of things that weren't there.
I'd push until my hands made
tiny fists.
I'd push until it was I who was sent
tumbling over the edge.

And then,
there they were again;
those distant, blurry figures
who seemed almost to float.
Whose blinding smiles
and outstretched arms
gave a new
false sense of security to
my broken little heart.

MY PAST

The past is the past
no matter how you look at it.
It happened,
there's no denying it.
People ask me,
"How are you so comfortable
sharing your story?"

My story
is a part of me,
and no matter how hard I try,
no matter how badly
I may want to,
I can't get rid of it.
So why not be okay with it?

Writing

"There is nothing to writing. All you do is sit down at a typewriter and bleed."

—Ernest Hemingway

WRITING

Writing began as an escape.
Now I can't live without it.
26 little letters became my world,
or more correctly,
all the worlds I've created.

MY SAVING GRACE

Every time
I hand you a poem
I'm handing you
a piece
of me.
Poetry is the only way
that I can express
my impending insanity.

Voice

Poetry isn't anything profound.
It's just words and feelings
on pieces of paper.

Paper

Paper is the only thing
that really understands me.
It doesn't judge the words
I write upon its surface.
It doesn't call me names
or tell me what I'm feeling is dumb.
It doesn't exclude me
and do the things
that people do,
and I think that's why I like it.

So, thank you, Paper,
for being the one thing
that's been there
through it all.

PRISONER

With every poem you write,
every masterpiece
you create,
the easier the words
start to flow,
the more of a prisoner
you'll become.

I'm a prisoner
to the pen,
a prisoner
to the paper.
Held captive
by the words
that have made their home
inside me.
They bang upon their cages,
begging to be let out,
begging to be freed,
but not everything in life
is free.

For me, writing started out as an escape. I've never been good at vocalizing how I feel. For the longest time, the only person I could depend on was myself. Opening up to people was something I didn't do. When things got rough, I pushed everything down. I was determined to not feel anything at all. Feelings just made everything worse. As I grew up, new feelings started to surface, and I did the same thing I'd always done: push them away and pretend they were not there. But after a while, that wasn't cutting it anymore. I was feeling too many things at the same time, and I was ready to blow. One tiny nudge, one more little mishap, was all it would take.

That's when I discovered writing. I sat down with a pen in my hand, hoping somehow to relieve the pain. It was almost as if my hand were doing the thinking instead of my brain. I wrote and wrote and wrote without stopping until all the hurt had left me, however briefly.

Writing's like a drug for me. It's something I know I couldn't live without. Every time I get frustrated, angry, sad, upset, I turn to pencil and paper. My world could be falling apart, the sky crashing to the ground, and all I have to do is scratch lines onto a piece of paper and everything is okay again.

At some point, though, I stopped writing because I wanted to and started writing because I needed to. My fingers would ache from gripping the pencil, but I *had* to write. I've become so dependent on words that they've become part of who I am. When I write, it's the only time I'm able to think freely. It's as if I've been doing this my whole life.

I used to think that I owned the words, but now I realize they own me. Without them to help me express myself, I'd be a helpless, hopeless blob of a human.

I've come to love words, and I believe that they, too, have come to love me.

Society

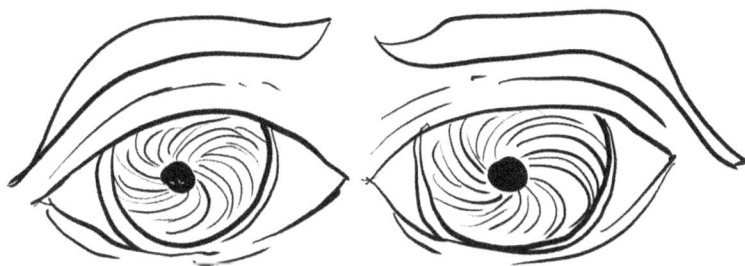

"Pretty"

Pretty: that's what I am.
The "pretty girl" is what I'm called.
I'm a pretty girl
with a pretty face,
yet they never seem to look beyond.
There's so much more to me.
Look for the deeper meaning.

Surface dwellers, otherwise known as players,
look at the face and go no deeper.
Surface dwellers disgust me.

My heart glows brighter than all my beauty combined
yet they still refuse to see it.
Overlooked, the heart is the simplest of things,
beating just for you.

"You're pretty."
Don't insult me.

So much of a person is defined by what they wear or how they look. If you don't follow the latest trends or wear your hair in a certain style, you're pegged as "uncool" or "weird." Labels are everywhere: on people, on things, on places. If you don't act like everyone else, you're labelled a misfit. Sad as it may be, most people only care about appearances, the sharpness of a jaw, the arch of an eyebrow, how thick your lips are. Nobody looks at the heart anymore. If the outside looks fine, it's assumed that the inside is fine, too. Many people wear masks to cover up who they are inside: people-pleasing chameleons that have changed color so many times they've forgotten their true shade.

People have always told me that I'm pretty, and for the most part, it's a compliment. But when people look only at the outside, that's when I get annoyed. This world is so caught up in appearances that people have forgotten how to feel, forgotten how to be human.

This world is full of people pleasers with low self-esteem, and I'm one of them. I want people to like me, and when they don't, it *kills* me inside. I, too, have gotten so caught up in appearances that I've forgotten that I wasn't like them. I was me. I was unique, and it was okay if not everyone in this world loved me.

So, next time you call somebody pretty, take a minute to stop and think about what exactly you're praising. Is it their face, or their heart? A lot of beautiful hearts go unnoticed because society has deemed them unworthy.

CHILDREN

They know nothing of the cruel world they live in.
They know nothing of the pain,
the tears,
the broken hearts.
They don't understand what it means to hurt,
to truly hurt.
They understand so little,
yet they are the lucky ones.
They have yet to be scarred by society.
They have yet to hear the ugly words
spat by hostile mouths.
Oh children,
they know nothing
of the cruel world they live in.

SOCIETY

People scare me.
They're all so trigger happy.
I don't want to die lonely
but I'm afraid of society.

They're so quick to judge.
They take one look at you and scoff.
But how little they know
about those around them.
If you had just reached out your hand,
we might've been friends
but no,
you had to judge.
You had to tell me just what you thought,
no matter if it hurt.
Only bullied for the laughs it got.
Now you'll never know.

Oh, how people scare me.
If they'd just put down their guns
we could all be happy.
This world is delirious,
yet I have to grow up in it.

"WELCOME TO SOCIETY"

"Welcome to society," they said, "Enjoy your stay."
No, I don't think I will,
not with everybody throwing their unwanted opinions my way.
You're expected
to conform to their rules,
be what they are,
but you can't be them if they're busy
being you.
They put on their masks each morning
and when they walk out the door,
they're no longer themselves
but puppets of the society they live in.
And the worst part is,
once you're here, you're here
to stay. There's no getting away.
"Welcome to society."

Internal Struggle

"I am left in a silent world with my silent thoughts banging around in my head."

—Bethany Wiggins, *Cured*

Pain

In the depths of my despair
I try to hold on to the light,
but all the goodness, the laughter
have gone.
I try, I try
to do it all right

but I do it all wrong.
What did I do to deserve this pain?
When did I lose my way?
Everything is torn from my grasp.
The devil laughs,
laughs at my pain.
I try to get up,
to brush it all off.
I'm carrying the weight of the world.
I stumble, I fall.
My cuts, they bleed
but my heart bleeds eternally.
I look to the future,
but I'm stuck in the past.

This pain wasn't meant to be endured,
but endure it I must.
I sit here in the darkness,
my punishment
till the end of time
wondering what could've been,
what might be.
If I lived twice
I'd mess it up again.
My wounds are fresh
but they are also old,
deep and scarred.

This is the story of my life
written page by page.
These monsters come
but they never go,
they make a home
inside me.

NOISE

Why am I so misunderstood?
Why do my words not come out clear?
Everything I say gets turned around,
and I say things even I don't want to hear.

There's a jumbled mess inside my head.
Full of disappointment, pain, and fear.
How do I get these things out?
How do I make it so they're just not there?

"Go away," I say.
"Go away!
Get out, get out, get out of my head!
I don't want you here.
Why won't you leave?"

Then the voices start.
I hear them loud and clear.
But don't be afraid,
don't be mistaken,
the voices represent the innermost parts of me.
The voices,
they're all me.

TRANSPARENT

Am I transparent,
see-through, clear?
It's almost as if I'm not even here.
Sometimes I wonder if anyone cares
that I am a girl: friendless, alone.
And sometimes I wonder if I had a clone,
would she be like me,
or popular like them?
Or would she be
as transparent
as me?

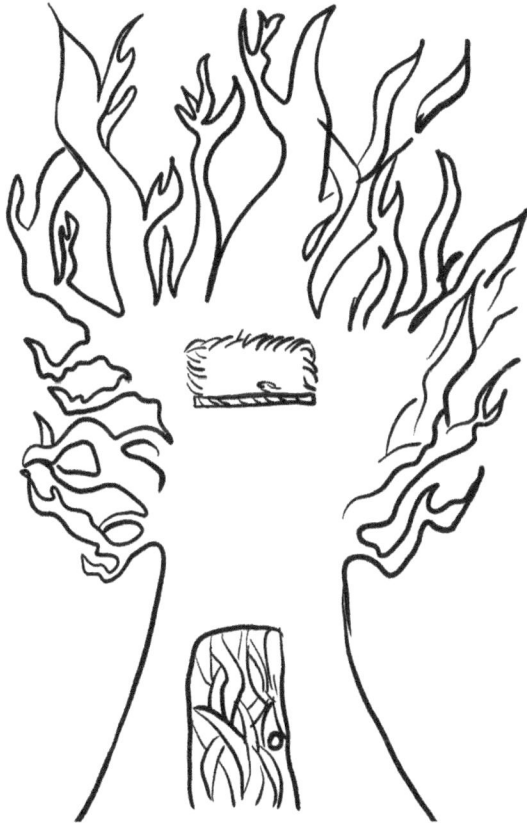

MISUNDERSTOOD

How do you cope
when someone thinks they know you
but they don't.
When someone says they understand,
but they're not even close.

I try,
I do,
but people say I don't.
How do they know what's inside my heart?
Apparently what I do is never enough
because I'm forced to give what I don't have.

My life has been a series of misfortunes.
Everything taken from me when I was weak,
when I couldn't fight,
when I couldn't win.
I'm not what I once was
still innocent maybe,
but with pain
a pro.
Misery and I are joined at the hip.
No, it'll never leave me be.

"What do you want from me?" I ask.
Will you answer
or leave me in chains?
No, you don't understand,
and you never will.
For I am different,
special is what I'm called.
Special, yes.

Who I Am Inside

A fire is raging inside my head,
one that I cannot put out.
It rages on,
and firefighters come,
but water will not quench it.

For it is the fire of my soul
fourteen years burning
and inside the flames dance my fears,
my insecurities,
and my worries.
I've tried to hide it,
to hide my fear,
but sometimes the memories sneak out my eyes and roll down
my cheeks,
bringing back the things I've tried so hard to forget.

I will it away
and wipe my tears.
I splash my face
and walk out of the room like nothing happened
and no one knows any better.

No Promises

Is it too much for you to be good?
Why do you do this to yourself,
knowing that each time you're digging the hole deeper?
You know how it's going to end,
but you let it go to your head.
You never change,
yet you promise yourself you will
and when all is said and done,
you end up in a worse state than before.

Mind shattered,
looking everywhere for the pieces,
and every time
you lose another part of the puzzle that is you.

So for once,
can't you just make yourself proud
and do the right thing?
"No promises," you'll tell yourself,
knowing that deep in your heart
you'll never be able to change.

ANXIETY

Gorgeous gowns.
But beneath my beauty
voices heave,
scream—
they tell me
I'm ugly.

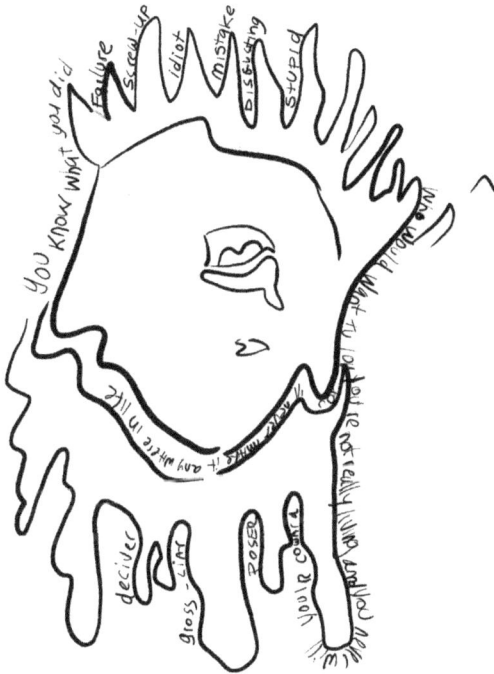

> "When I had nothing to lose, I had everything. When I stopped being who I am, I found myself."
>
> —**Paulo Coelho**, *Eleven Minutes*

The voices have always been there. Not so much out-loud voices as inner whispers. And they're not exactly easy to shut off. I can't just press the mute button.

No matter how often people may tell me that I'm pretty, or that I'm beautiful, it's always been kind of hard to believe. If you grew up believing that grass is black, it'd be pretty hard to convince you that it's actually green, right? Same goes for me. I spent the early years of my life feeling as though I'd never be pretty enough, good enough, happy enough for anyone, and a few people saying otherwise didn't make it true.

Over the years I've come to learn that those voices, those doubts, are lies. Learning how to shut them out has been a process, and occasionally (like on the day I wrote "Anxiety"), I slip and let them back in. But to err is human, and I am unfailingly human in every way.

Now, when I look in the mirror and hear those whispers, I remind myself that I'm human. I'm not perfect, and that's okay.

WALLS

The look in her eyes,
that deep, celestial blue,
reminds you of a child
who's just been given
a birthday balloon.
Mischievously glinting,
they seem almost
to taunt you,
willing you closer.

There's a mystery to her,
something you can't quite
understand.
You try to delve deeper
but are knocked
flat on your back,
gasping for air;
you seem to have hit a wall
that wasn't there before.

Walls are built
to keep people out
but also
to keep people in
and you're beginning to wonder
which one it is.

FURIES OF OLD

Furies of old
circle my heart,
the chains they wrought
binding tighter.
My Elysium
is but a dream,
for it is a place
only heroes see.
I am not a hero
but a monster,
so ugly,
grotesque,
so immensely repulsive
that the Fields of Punishment
are my only option.
My appearance
is beautiful,
or so everyone tells me,
but if they could look inside,
see the interior of my heart,
walk these hallways
and open these doors,
their opinion would change
quite quickly,
of that
I am sure.

HIDING FROM TRUTH

I have a problem.
Many, to be honest,
but there's one I'm quite worried about.
It's second nature,
something I don't think about.

To lie is easier than to tell the truth.
It's the first thing out of my mouth,
it's never been hard.
I guess that says something about me.

What if people don't know me?
What if my lies have become my truth?
What if I have lost the ability to distinguish
fact from fiction?
Yes,
I have a problem,
and I don't know how to fix it.

PITY PARTY

I yell, I cry,
I scream, I lie.
Everything a good girl shouldn't do.
I'm a disappointment to myself.
I said I'd get better,
be better,
feel better,
yet I seem to make myself worse.

Why am I who I am?
Why can't I be someone better?
All I seem to do is let people down.
I disappoint,
I tear things apart
when all I want is to build them up.
You can't grow to be something
when you already amount to nothing.

This has turned into a pity-party poem,
so this is where I'll say my goodbyes.

Sighs
Waves goodbye

THIS IS FOREVER

This is *not* goodbye forever,
just until I'm better.

Oh, why did I think I'd be able
to do this?

STILL CRYING EVERY NIGHT

I'm back and better than ever,
at least that's what I'd say
if I weren't still
crying every night.

All the Things I Don't Know How to Say

I'm afraid of love. I'm afraid of being loved. I'm afraid *to* love. Everything gets twisted around in my head. The things I want to say, I can't; and the things I don't want to say, I do. I *want* people to understand me. I *want* to open up, but so many of the people I've opened up to have manipulated me and wrapped me around their little finger. They've used my insecurities and fears for their own personal gain. They didn't want me for my friendship, they wanted me because they got something out of me. When I stopped being useful, when they got bored, they simply threw me away, and it never once seemed to bother them. It was almost as if they couldn't see that I was a person, too.

It's scary, trusting people. I want to believe that it'll be different, that this new person won't hurt me too. But I can't ever know that for sure. I've been wrong so many times. I've been promised all types of things: they'll never hurt me, they'll always be there, they'll never let anyone else hurt me, they're different, they're not like everyone else. And every time, I fall for their lies. I've gotten so wrapped up in trying to make the people I care about happy that I've almost lost myself completely. I give up pieces of me to make them whole, and when all's said and done, I end up more broken than when I started.

When I open up to somebody, I feel as if I'm giving them a piece of me. I'm trusting that they'll hold me carefully and not walk away with my heart beating in their hands. So many people have walked away, and they've never returned to me what I so graciously let them have.

I'm one giant jigsaw puzzle, depleted of the pieces that make me whole.

I once read that the heart is like a broken glass: you can glue the pieces back together, but you'll always be able to see the cracks.

That's something most people don't understand. They don't see me as broken. I've become so good at gluing myself back together, then hiding the cracks as best I can. My friends admire my fearlessness; they admire my confidence. They've told me that they want to someday be as confident as I am. They see the confident, happy kid who's got it all together, but they don't see what I'm hiding. One of my biggest fears is that eventually people will see me the way I see myself. They'll see me for the broken person I am and decide that I'm not worth the effort.

But here's the thing: I'm tired of hiding. I'm tired of being "fearless" and "confident." For once, I don't want to be the kid that everyone leans on, the one that fixes everyone else's problems. I'm tired of being strong. For once, I want to be weak. I want to lean on somebody else. Even though being strong is a part of who I am, I can't be strong forever. Everyone breaks eventually.

But maybe I'm not broken. Maybe I'm not the person I think I am. Maybe I *am* the happy, confident girl that everyone sees. Maybe I'm being too hard on myself.

But unlike everyone else, I don't love myself—not yet. I'm still learning. I'll get there eventually.

The last time I checked, broken crayons still color.

AFRAID

She's afraid to let someone in
afraid to fall under the crashing waves again.

Remembering what it feels like to drown
not to know which way is up or down
to let out a scream of utter terror
only to be silenced by a beast that's not there.

She's afraid of the pain
the rejection.
She's afraid of being alone
confused
not knowing which way
will take her home.

It's Only in My Head

Afraid to love,
afraid of rejection,
afraid of the things that aren't there,

like monsters in the closet,
monsters under the bed,
monsters in places that are
only in my head.
Like the monster I named Fear,
like an imaginary friend,
it exists only up there.

But now I've got the monsters in cages,
determined not to let them escape,
determined to keep myself sane.

"It's only pretend," I tell myself.
"It's only in my head."

We all have our demons. Every single one of us struggles with something. Whether it's pride, self-esteem, anxiety, self-doubt, depression... it's there, and there's no denying it. Sure, we can *pretend* it's not there. We can push it away to the deepest, darkest part of our soul, but eventually it'll resurface. It always does. In the words of Albus Dumbledore, "Numbing the pain for a while will make it worse when you finally feel it."

These problems, they haunt us. Like ghosts, they're always there. Sitting, waiting, watching. Bottling it up and pretending that nothing's wrong doesn't work. Take it from me. I have severe ADHD. I either hyperfocus or don't focus at all. So when life throws me a curveball, I can't dodge it, try as I might. I slip back into old habits and start to worry. And worry. And worry. No matter what I do, it almost always ends up consuming me.

As hard as I've tried to break it, this cycle repeats. I became tired, so very tired, of going through the same motions over and over again. One day I sat back and asked myself, "Why do I worry so much when there's nothing I can do?"

That was the day I realized that this fear, this pain, this worry, only hurts if I let it. I realized that these problems, my demons, were nothing but figments of my imagination. I was obsessing over something insignificant and had blown it completely out of proportion.

And the demons? They were only in my head. I had put them there, and I could just as easily make them leave. Our worst enemies will always be the monsters we create, but we don't have to be afraid anymore; not as long as we remember...

It's only in our head.

THE ATTIC

My brain is an attic
filled with all sorts of things.
Dusty boxes
sealed with tape
packed away.

The fan's broken
the lightbulb's burned out
and when it goes dark
the monsters come out.

They toss around my boxes
cause chaos and wreak havoc.
They play games
and do terrible things.
They rip the tape
off my Pandora's box.

When childhood innocence
comes out to play,
its laughter echoing off the walls of my brain,
it frolics, it jumps,
it stomps and it screams,
and then it falls to the floor,
all happiness ripped from its seams.

So I hurry, I scurry
to the attic in my head.
I replace the bulb
and turn on the light.
Monsters can't
thrive in the day,
they are creatures of the night.

I stuff everything back
into boxes,
seal them with tape,
and pack them away.

Because my brain is an attic
filled with all sorts of things,
things I think I cherish,
and things I can't bear
to lose.

I Don't Dream

My brain is a wild place
full of wild thoughts
beyond my comprehension.
And when at night
I close my eyes,
the pictures appear
like a ghostly TV
with no screen.
Sometimes pleasant,
sometimes not,
are the ideas
that flutter
behind my eyelids.
Their wings like those of a butterfly:
fragile, soft;
if I move too quickly
they disappear.
I'm haunted by the memories
of the life I once lived,
of all the places I've been,
of the people
I once considered
precious.
Reminders of a life
I'll never have
and of all the people
I'll never be.
I open my eyes
and take note
of the tears gliding silently
down my cheeks,
and I remind myself
not to dream.

DREAMS

Everything I am is built upon dreams.
If I didn't have my dreams,
what would I be?
Reality sucks, it gets worse by the day.
I lay down my head
and it all goes away.

I hate to wake up and look in the mirror
and see the person I have become.
I want to be better,
so I dream that I am.

A dream is a wish,
so if dreams can come true, then I'll wish upon a star,
and when I wake up and realize that I'm still the same,
that the scars will never go away,
I'll dream of something better.
I'll dream of a place where I can be me
and be loved for every scar on my body,
for every scar etched into my brain.
I'll realize that the scars made me the dreamer I am.
I can't change my reality,
but I can change the way I see it.

STITCHES

Stitches and stitches
around my heart.
Stitches and stitches
scar my heart.
Those faint white lines
mar the beauty
of my aorta.
My heart used to do so many things,
now it only pumps blood.
Once a crimson wonder,
now black and blue,
it only beats because it has to.
If you're like me,
it shatters easily.
It's such an unpredictable thing,
it feels what it wants,
and when all is said and done,
it breaks again
because it was convinced
that this love
was the last one.

Stitches and stitches
surround my heart.
Stitches and stitches
scar my heart.
I'm a monster
of the Frankenstein type,
and oh, what I wouldn't have given
to have never been
brought to life.

I have scars, outside and in, ones you can see and ones you can't. I have learned that the worst scars are almost always on the inside, in places no one can reach, places no one can see.

We hurt in places no one can fix us. We use metaphors to describe our pain. We're always "breaking" or "falling apart." We're "dying" or "splintering." Our pain doesn't exist outside of metaphors, outside of words. We feel that we have to name our hurt in order to justify it, to make it real.

We are a mass of scars, a lump of bruises. We are a Frankensteinian nightmare. A mesh of parts.

We are what we make of ourselves, and we are what others have made us be. We are made of those who have built and broken us. We are the ivory tower with its glistening stones, but we are also the princess trapped inside.

Stitches and stitches
around my heart.
Stitches and stitches
scar my heart.

Some people don't realize that the words they use, the metaphorical daggers they throw, hurt. Other people just don't care. They want to watch the world burn. They take pleasure in watching others bleed. They punch just so they can watch the marks appear, just so they can watch us turn black and blue. They delight in the pain of others, but can't stand their own. To them, it's bully or be bullied. To them, it's hurt or be hurt.

But what they don't know is that we're used to this. We've been torn down before. We've been stripped of everything that makes us human. We know how true pain feels. We've looked fear in the face. We've stared straight into its beady little eyes.

They don't scare us.
They don't scare me.
They are nothing but pinpricks of unhappiness, a tsunami in a baby pool.
They can't drown me.

At one point, sure, their words may have stung. I may have, at one point, valued their opinion, even sought it. It would have killed me when they feigned indifference, when they walked away. I may have cared then, but I don't now.

They won't leave marks, not anymore.

You Are Loved

You were born into a world of hate
and deception. The sun
may seem to shine less brightly here
and the stars to be crashing down from above,
but don't let them get to you,
don't let them fill your head with lies.
Don't let them tell you you're worth nothing,
because that's when the madness starts.

"For we are God's masterpiece, created in Christ Jesus to do good works, which God prepared in advance for us to do."

—Ephesians 2:10

Lies & Broken Promises

"What a treacherous thing it is to believe that a person is more than a person."

—John Green, *Paper Towns*

My Story

Your first mistake was making me
perfect. You can't see my demons,
only my halo.

I took down my walls.
I let you in.
I thrived, then I died.
You took my soul and crushed it in the palm of your hand,
left me bleeding,
mind swirling,
stomach in knots.
You never felt my pain.
To you it was all a game,
a game only you knew how to play.
I gave you my heart but you turned on me.
You played me like a violin.
You told me I was your everything
but in the end, I was nothing.

Don't take love from strangers. Lesson learned.
Monsters don't live under the bed,
they live inside our head,
tearing us apart
and telling us things that just aren't true.

These are my demons
and this is my story.
I used to love
I used to be content.
I gave you everything
then you tossed me aside.
You did this to me,
I hope you're happy.

Dear Childhood Friend,

You were my first real friend. Before you, the only person I could rely on was myself. Everybody else had let me down. I was never intent on making friends because I knew that I'd end up moving again. If I was going to leave them eventually, what was the point? But when you walked into my life, there wasn't much I could do to keep you out.

We met in first grade. It was story time, and we ended up next to each other on the rug. I had on these little red, white, and blue bracelets, and you wanted one. When you asked me for one, I said no. I had just gotten them and wanted to keep them. You told me that friends share, and I remember looking at you in complete amazement. I had never had a friend before, and here you were, calling me yours. You promised that if I gave you one we'd be best friends forever. I was awestruck. I'd never had a "best" friend. I hurriedly took off one of my bracelets and gave it to you. That night, I could barely sleep. All I could think about was you and how we'd be best friends forever.

We were practically inseparable. We did everything to-gether: skipped hand in hand down the hallways, danced barefoot on the lunch tables after school, played hide-and-go-seek in the library, whispered secrets to each other in the bathroom, caught grasshoppers at recess on the playground, played house, sang along at the top of our lungs to "Wrecking Ball" in the computer lab, had two-hour phone calls almost every day after school, and wrote mounds of bucket papers to each other in fourth grade.

At your ninth birthday party, one of the girls made me cry. (I always have been the sensitive type.) I ran into your bedroom and locked the door. You yelled at her, told her that nobody talks to your best friend that way and that you couldn't believe she would do that, and if she was going to be rude like that to your best friend at your birthday party, then she could leave. If she didn't like me, then she didn't like you. You were my protector, my champion.

In fifth grade, you promised me you'd always be there. You told me you'd never let anybody hurt me, that you'd always stand up for me. I remember smiling at you, tears in my eyes, believing that I had struck gold. You even pinky promised.

Sixth grade came. Not only were we starting middle school, we were starting it at a new school. I was scared, and you told me that we'd get through it together. But middle school got to you. There were new kids, popular kids, and you wanted to be noticed. So you decided that if you were going to be popular, you couldn't be friends with me. You stopped hanging out with me, stopped talking to me, even started avoiding me altogether. It was only when you had no one else to hang out with that you even acknowledged me. But I ignored all that, because in the end, you were still my best friend.

I was loyal. So loyal. No matter how much you made fun of me, ignored me, made up rumors about me, laughed at me, I convinced myself that you still loved me. Even when you ditched me, no matter how clear you made it, I still came crawling back to you on my hands and knees. You were all I had ever known. I didn't want another best friend. I wanted you. Even as I cried myself to sleep at night, I still somehow convinced myself that you'd come back to me. You had to. We were best friends forever. You'd promised.

But promises meant nothing to you. It was almost as if you thrived on my pain. You stabbed me in the back, time after time. And what did I do? Like an idiot, I crawled back to you, begging for your friendship. You'd smile that sickly sweet smile, tell me that you were sorry, and promise me best friends forever. I was so naive.

I would go to my mother's English classroom during lunch or at recess and cry. I didn't tell her what was going on for the longest time—how could I explain to her that my first friend, my best friend, no longer wanted me, that she hated me? I was so scared, because I knew I was losing you, and I wasn't ready to lose someone else. And just like everybody else, you had promised to love me and then tossed me out like I had never meant anything to you. I cried. So much. All I wanted was my best friend back. I prayed to God. I even wished on stars. But some people aren't meant to be in your life forever, not even if they promise.

When I moved, you didn't even say goodbye. For the first four or five months, I talked to no one. I didn't want friends. To me, everybody was the same; they were all backstabbing liars, and I wanted no part in it. I had put up all these walls. I promised myself that I would never let anybody else in. I was scared, because if I couldn't trust you, then whom could I trust?

The truth is, you didn't just break me, you shattered me. I realize now that you weren't a best friend at all. Best friends don't manipulate each other. They don't ditch each other when things aren't working out. They stick up for each other and hurt with each other. They never let each other feel alone, especially not in times of need. When I needed you, you weren't there. You were off gallivanting with your new, better friends.

It took me a long time to let you go. I held on to all that pain you had inflicted upon me for so long. After I let you go, I was able to let new people in. Better people. The friends I have now, I would give them the moon if they asked for it. Not only do I love them with everything I am, but they love me, too. You showed me what kind of friend not to be.

Now you're just somebody that I used to know.

> "When someone leaves, it's because someone else is about to arrive."
>
> —Paulo Coelho, *The Zahir*

Your ex-best friend,

Priscilla Johnson

HUMAN

Can you see me over here?
Can you see me through the tears?
Black streaks match the mood of my heart,
smeared makeup inspires my art.

Can you see me over here
through the veil that hides my fear?
I'm dead inside because of you,
because you think I'm bulletproof.

What am I to you?
I'm only human.

RAPUNZEL

Lies, lies,
that's all you know.
One moment you say you love me,
the next you're cutting me down.
Lies, lies,
that's who you are.
One moment you're here,
the next you're out the door.

You've got me wrapped around your little finger
but you can't keep me locked up anymore.
You've got me wrapped around your little finger
and you're holding me tight.

You've got mc locked up,
let me go.
Let down your hair
and let me go.

Someone like Me

Where did I lose you?
Where did it all go wrong?
I should've held on better,
but I let go
and now you're gone.

Falling, falling,
I'm spiraling out of control.
Have I lost you forever?
I never meant to let you go.

Find someone like me
that'll hold on tight.
That'll give you something I couldn't,
that'll hold your heart.

Find someone like me.
I'm a thousand miles away
and I've missed my chance.

A Cycle

I don't understand,
what did I do?
All I did was pledge myself to you.
You were happy for a bit,
and then you moved on,
with my heart in your pocket.

I trusted you when I didn't trust myself,
thinking that somehow
you would make me better,
when in reality
you only made me worse.

You turned a hundred broken pieces
into a thousand.
Now it's all just a downward spiral,
I couldn't help it if I tried.

I'm stuck inside my own head,
slowly tearing myself apart.
My heart is turning black and blue,
it's a battle to stay alive.

Dear Eleven-Year-Old Me

Life will get better,
trust me.
You don't have to die
you don't have to cry.
Stop trying to drown yourself in the bathtub.
Just because she doesn't like you
just because she bullies you
just because she doesn't care
doesn't mean you shouldn't, too.

Dear eleven-year-old me,
you'll learn to love yourself
eventually.

This Is Me

I'm sorry if you don't like who I've become.
Once I may have taken
your words to heart
and dwelled on them day and night,
wondering what I could do to make you like me.
But now I see your betrayal for what it is:

I lost someone who didn't care
and you lost someone who did.

Disabilities

"It is better to be hated for what you are than loved for what you are not."

—André Gide, Autumn Leaves

My little sister drowned on a beautiful summer day. Like most memories from when I was young, it's not a memory at all—I was only told about it. I imagine the day was pretty because not many people go swimming in Pennsylvania otherwise. Marie had her whole life ahead of her. By societal standards, she was perfect. It's remarkable just how many blemishes your body can acquire after being dead for ten minutes. By the grace of God, she came back to life. For my sister and me, this is where our story begins.

We were still living with our biological parents. I know they were there. I know I was there. I know my five-year-old and four-year-old brothers were there. I've pieced together small snippets of stories over the years. It's those little snippets of truth that fill these pages. I don't know much, but I do know she drowned in a kiddy pool. I know that my brothers and my dad were standing in the front yard watching motorcycles go by. My sister and I were with my mom when our mother decided that she had to use the restroom. She took me with her and left Marie outside. "Marie never goes near the pool" was her excuse. I don't really know how it happened, but my little sister ended up in the water. My oldest brother tried to save her. He was the first to turn around after the motorcycles had passed. He saw her lying facedown in the pool and screamed.

Nobody was even watching her. My brother found Marie and pulled her out of the water. He was too late. I mean, nobody can blame him; he was five. It's amazing, though, that my five-year-old brother had the intelligence to realize something was wrong. It's incredible that he tried to save her.

Our father must have gone into a rage when he found out because he actually punched my five-year-old brother in the face. Why would he do that? It makes no sense. Was he punching him for trying to save her? I'll never know. From what I've heard, he did try to administer CPR, but she was unresponsive. The neighbors heard my brother's scream and called the police. I don't know who saved my sister, and my dad ended up in jail, not for child neglect but for assault. The rest of us got to learn about foster care and just how awful life can be.

I've shared some of my foster-care story already. My sister has another one, and it deserves to be told. When the doctors brought her back, she wasn't the same. The prognosis was that she'd never be able to do anything on her own and would never leave a wheelchair. If the brain is deprived of oxygen for more than four to six minutes, a child may permanently lose basic functions and may even require lifelong care. The disruption of brain cells may cause memory loss, learning disabilities, and loss of motor functions. Since her heart stopped beating for ten minutes, this is what she faced.

Although my sister suffered a traumatic brain injury, she has accomplished far more than anyone thought possible. Within one month of the accident, Marie was assigned foster parents who stayed with her, worked with her, and did everything in their power to help her become as independent as possible. For a while her traumatic brain injury left her paralyzed. The only movements she made were involuntary. She could wiggle a little bit and roll her head. She couldn't eat. Everything she consumed was pureed and fed directly to her stomach through a feeding tube. Her drinks had to be thickened, because she was at risk of silent asphyxiation and could choke without anyone knowing.

My two brothers and I were in foster care together for a short while following our sister's near drowning. We were eventually separated, and I ended up in the same foster home as my little sister. Not for very long, though. I survived ten more after that, some far worse than others. At least Marie got to stay in her new home forever.

It's still difficult to believe that strangers open their homes to children that aren't their own. Some of these people are horrible, but the majority of them mean well, and quite a few of them are extraordinary people led by the Holy Spirit who have reached nothing short of sainthood. Most foster parents I know about and have lived with at least cared about me and the other children they welcomed more than my own parents did. My biological parents were careless and, from what I have been told, were dealing with substance abuse. They either didn't know how to take care of us or didn't want to. At least, not badly enough to get clean. So here I am.

I still talk to Marie. We have a bond that can never be broken. She is, in so many ways, my other half. Her family is raising her as well as they can, and she is doing amazingly considering what she's been through. We owe everything, all of her progress, to God and the support of her foster parents.

THE DISABLED GIRL

I'm two thousand miles away
and incapable of doing anything
to help the little girl
who has my heart,
who is my world.
I sit on the other end of the phone
and hear the little girl laugh.
Then the girl tells me that she's scared of the people
she has no choice but to deal with.
They laugh,
they mock,
they point,
and they stare.
"These people were my friends," she whispers,
"but no one wants to hang out
with the disabled girl."

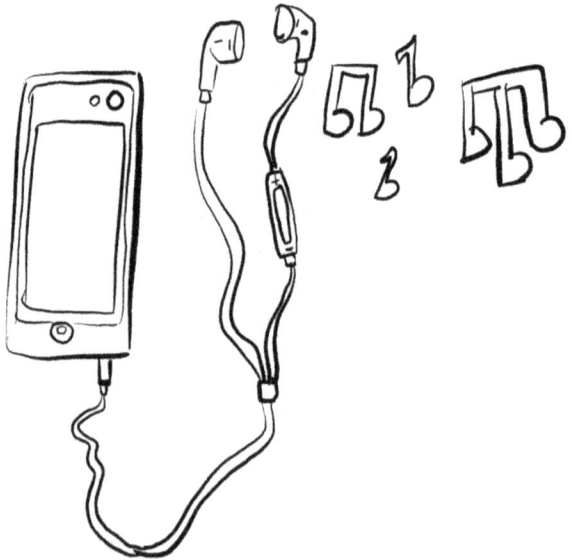

"Perfect"

She was different,
special,
one of a kind.
The other girls were all the same,
made of plastic,
hiding who they were to become:
society's version of
"perfect."
When the girl who is different
comes into contact
with "Barbies,"
they tear her down
because she threatens their
normality.
They are plastic
and she is real.
They are jealous
because she is so good
at being herself,
and they are failing so hard
at trying to be
someone else.

You're my Love Song

The Phone Call

"I don't want to be who I am."
She trembles.
She's so young,
so precious,
yet she already knows what it feels like
to be unwanted,
for people to point at her and laugh
all because she's "different."

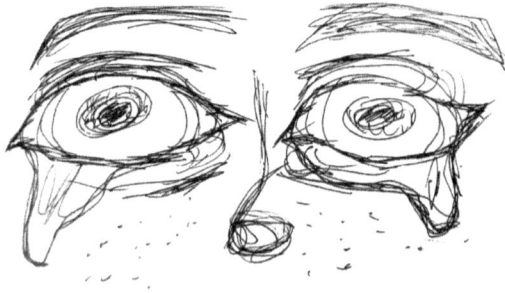

Dear Little Sister,

I know what they say. I know what you believe. I know
that words sting, and that people can be mean. They don't
see you for who you are. They see what's on the outside, not
what's on the inside. They can't see your heart.

I can.

I know you better than you may think. I know that, in
many ways, you're just like me. You're not like them.
You never will be.

Love,

Your built-in best friend

"Just because your version of
normal isn't the same as someone
else's version doesn't mean that
there's anything wrong with you."

—John Boyne,
The Terrible Thing That Happened to Barnaby Brocket

More Lies & Broken Promises

"I have given away my whole soul to someone who treats it as if it were a flower to put in his coat."

—Oscar Wilde, *The Picture of Dorian Gray*

THE DEMON

You feel the pain,
it's not as much inside
as all over.
It fills every crack and crevice.
The enemy whispers, lies inside your head,
tells you that you're not good enough.
But, you say, *who is the enemy*
when the only person bringing me down is me?
I am the enemy.
I am the mistake.
You fill your head with lies.
How can I not, you think,
when there's nothing left to love?

This is the problem,
this is the issue.
It is not you
but the demon that has made its home inside you.
You can't let it bring you down.

As long as you live,
and breathe,
fight the demon that dwells within.
You are not the demon,
the demon does not define you.
You are more than the demon will ever be.

Don't fight it with knives,
don't fight it with razors,
don't mark your body trying to show it who's better.
That's what it wants,
it lives for the pain.
Every time you cut,
it wins.

But the fight isn't over,
the battle isn't won,
it's you versus the demon inside.
I believe in you,
I'll fight by your side.
As long as you let me, I'll be there.

Right now,
all you can see is
the endless abyss;
but I see the light,
the flowers blooming
inside your chest.

So, don't try to fight it,
become one with it.
Be okay with the pain you feel.
Let it become part of you,
part of your story,
a story that you'll one day be able to tell.

I wrote this poem for a friend who was going through a hard time. She hated herself. She'd cut with knives, with razors, with whatever was available. It'd leave huge, ugly marks on her skin, scars that someday she'd regret having made.

I tried to build her up, tried to let her know that she was wanted, that she was loved. I'd write her letters reminding her of all the beauty that lived inside her.

I compared the pain she was feeling with that of a demon. This demon represented her pain, her fear, her anxiety. It represented the voices, the what-ifs that crept into her head at night.

What if no one loves me?

What if no one cares?

What if I cut just one more time? Will it make the pain go away?

These voices, I'm sad to say, won. She didn't stop cutting, and as far as I know, she still does. Self-harm became her way of dealing with the pain. She was so unhappy. Nobody should have to live like that: filled with anger, pain, and fear.

I'm telling you this so you don't fall down the same rabbit hole. I thought I could help her because I've fallen down that hole, too. I hated myself. It wasn't my body that was the problem, but what was inside my body. The brain, just like any other organ, can get sick. I rationalized, told myself that cutting was okay. I was tired of people thinking that I had it all together, tired of people seeing me as pretty. I figured that if I was ugly on the inside, I had to be ugly on the outside, too. I needed them to see that I wasn't okay.

I was so wrong. I stopped cutting, but only because somebody asked me to, and it was someone I wouldn't in a million years have imagined caring about what I did to my body. He almost seemed hurt by the fact that I hated myself. He acted as if those angry red lines offended him. If *he* cared, then who else did?

The voices that say you're not enough, that you're ugly, that you're stupid, are liars. Don't do what I did; don't believe them. You ARE beautiful, you ARE smart, you ARE enough. If you are living, if you are breathing, it's because you were meant to be here. God made you, shaped you with His own two hands. God doesn't make mistakes. If He says that you are enough, believe Him. He knows.

So, the next time the demons start whispering, filling your head with lies, remember that God made you, and God doesn't make mistakes.

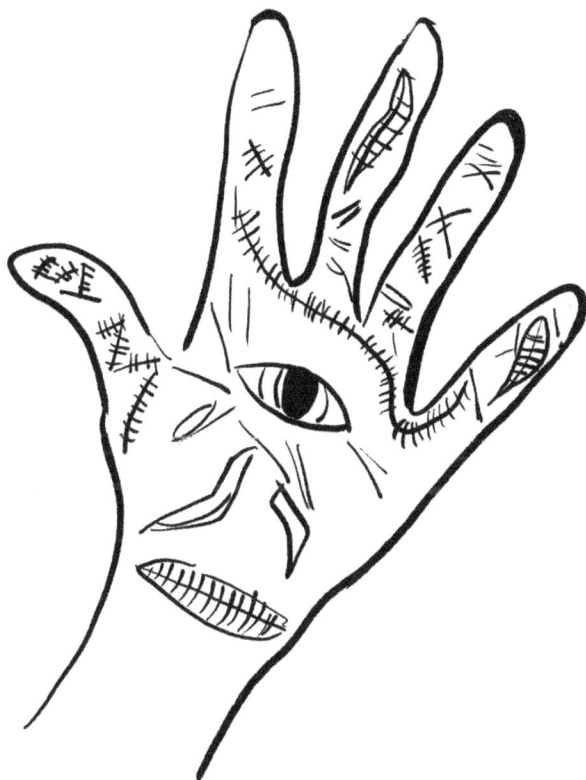

I SEE ALL

INCOMPLETE

Nobody listens.
Why do I give advice if nobody cares?
By making them better
I've broken me down.
I've given up pieces of me to make them whole.
And this is how they thank me?

Left to Wonder

Thinking people are talking
behind your back.
Never knowing what they're saying,
or whether it's over.
Wishing you could hear their thoughts,
but you can't.
So, you're left to wonder
if they really like you or not.

SLITHER

I had your back
I held you up
became your armor
and took all those bullets for you.
I was the rock
you built all your lies upon
and in your grasp
I slowly withered
weakening
by the day.

Like poison
you contaminated me
my sense of who I was
without you
fading
your fangs
plunged right in
cut off all oxygen
to my brain.

When I finally broke free
I felt the poison ebb away.
You were poisonous
venomous
practically heartless
and yet
I willingly believed every lie you told.

The truth is
you're a snake.
So go ahead
slither away.

ALL YOU NEEDED WAS LOVE

I was young,
naive,
and believed you when
you said you cared.
Like a dog
I obeyed your orders,
and like a soldier
I fought by your side.
Your words were arrows
you fired at
my heart.
Your actions were knives
you drove into
my back.

My ever-growing
military might,
and all the weapons
you left imbedded,
never seemed to bother you,
you never seemed to care
that I was dying slowly
from the poisoned tips
of your arrows.
You'd attack
without warning,
then play victim,
pretending to wither like a flower,
begging to be watered because
"all you needed was love."

I don't believe the whole "respect is earned" thing. From the minute I met you, you had my respect. What you said and did after that determined whether or not you kept it.

You didn't.

I liked you at first. I really did. We were so much alike: weird, loud, crazy, fun. Our classmates thought we had been best friends forever, when in fact I had just met you that year. We were closer than sisters.

When life started to beat you up, you looked to me for help. If I'm anything, it's loyal. I promised that you weren't going to hurt alone. I wouldn't allow it. I knew how it felt to be alone, to have no one. It's a horrible feeling, and I never once wished that upon you.

I did everything I could to make you better. I wrote you letters, smiled, laughed, and talked with you every day. I made sure you were included. I tried my hardest to glue your broken pieces back together, but every time I'd start something good, you'd tear it down. You started putting up all these walls. You were impenetrable. You would beg, plead, implore me to help, but you wouldn't let me in. You pushed me away. You wouldn't even let me try. Then you'd yell at me, mad that I wasn't there to catch you when you fell. But how could I have been? It was a game of cat and mouse. No matter how hard the cat tried, he could never win.

You lied. About so many things. You lied to get attention, you lied to make me feel bad.

You cut to get my attention. I mean, how warped is that? I went to bed every night worried. For you. I woke up every morning wondering if you were doing the same.

Were you really suicidal?

Or was it just another lie, another of your cruel little jokes?

Whatever it was, it wasn't funny. I used to cry—over you. You'd ignore me for a week, sometimes two, seemingly for no reason, and then suddenly we were friends again.

I tried to ignore it all. You needed me, or so you made me believe. I couldn't let you hurt alone.

You cut every day, made suicidal jokes, said you wanted to die. You even acted like you truly meant it, like you were flashing us all some sign, like you were begging to be saved.

You didn't want to be saved.

I loved you as much as I could. I tried to let you know that I cared.

You picked fights with other kids. I ignored it.
You always had a new boyfriend. I ignored it.

You started talking behind my back, saying that I was the fake one, that I was the one with the ego. You said I was the attention seeker, a teacher's pet, that I got special attention. None of it was true.

I can't say I wasn't warned. People told me you were a heartbreaker. I told them they were wrong. I stood up for you.

I should have listened. If I had, maybe you wouldn't have broken my heart, too.

I hope your happy ending is with someone who will make you better, someone who can do the job I failed to finish. I hope you end up happy.

"Forgiving isn't something you do for someone else. It's something you do for yourself. It's saying, You're not important enough to have a stranglehold on me. It's saying, You don't get to trap me in the past. I am worthy of a future."

—Jodi Picoult, The Storyteller

See ya on the flip side,

Priscilla

Mema

Because of Cancer

She shouldn't be in bed.

She should be out shopping
instead. But she's in bed
because of cancer.
She should be making breakfast
but instead she's in bed
because of cancer.
Her hair should grow back
yet it won't
because of cancer.
She shouldn't be throwing up
yet she is
because of cancer.
The doctors say she's better
she doesn't believe them
because of cancer.
It racks her body
every breath is painful
because of cancer.
She wants to be happy
but doesn't know how.
She says she's dying
the radiation hurts
she can't sleep
won't eat
is depressed
and it's all because of cancer.
"Get better," I plead.
She smiles and closes her eyes.
"I'm trying."
She wants to give up
because of cancer.

My grandmother was the absolute light of my life. She was a burning lighthouse in a sea of infinite darkness. I never had much until I had her. One person can truly make all the difference. She told me once that I had stolen a piece of her heart, and until she passed, I didn't realize that she had stolen a piece of mine, too. She had never treated me as less than her granddaughter, her very own flesh and blood. She had loved me with *every single inch* of her heart. I have yet to meet a woman with a bigger heart.

She radiated love and joy.

Until I was seven, I didn't have a real family. So when I finally got one, I naively believed that they'd never leave me, not even in death.

I wrote "Because of Cancer" about a month before my grandmother passed. At the time she was still going through chemo, but her strength and health were deteriorating so quickly that the doctors stopped her treatment.

It was becoming difficult for her to get out of bed. She refused to eat, claiming that the food wouldn't stay down. She became aggressively thin. Her hair was falling out in clumps. But despite it all, I still believed that she would get better. She *had* to. I couldn't bear the thought of being without her.

My grandmother had never been the type of woman to give up on something. She was the strongest woman I knew and would do whatever it took to make sure her family was happy.

At one point I pulled a chair into her room, sat beside her bed, and gently took one of her puffy, swollen hands in mine. Her breathing had become extremely heavy, and it took her a few seconds to register that I was there. I started telling her about all the things we'd do together when she got better. I told her that her doctors said she was getting stronger and that she'd be up and walking in no time. She just shook her head and told me that the doctors were liars. She wasn't going to get better. I protested, telling her that she had to get better. I *needed* her. She turned her head and looked at me, and all the joy I remembered, all the happiness, was gone. I had never seen fear in her eyes, and it terrified me. Her gaze locked onto mine. She squeezed my hand and whispered, "I'm sorry, sweetie. I'm not going to get better. I'm dying of cancer." She relaxed her grip and turned her eyes back to the ceiling.

When I wrote that poem, I was angry. So angry. I was losing my grandmother, and it was all because of cancer. There was no reason why a woman of such beauty and grace should have to slowly suffer, knowing that every day she was closer to death. She couldn't bear the idea of dying that way. She didn't want anybody to know. She made us promise that we would tell nobody, not even her closest friends.

I believe that she was a lot like me. She refused to believe something bad could happen to her or to the people she loved. She tried to block it out, pretend that she was okay, but at one point, she just couldn't ignore it anymore. She fought for as long as she could—for us, her family. She didn't want to leave.

Cancer may have physically taken my grandmother, but it can never take the memories we made, and it can never take the love that she so freely gave.

Cancer does not define her.

I WILL ♥ ALWAYS LOVE YOU

CANCER

Cancer took the one I loved,
the one who still believed in me.
No matter how much I let her down,
she never doubted I could fix it.

Cancer took the one I loved,
the one who always saw the best in me.
She was supposed to get better
but cancer took her,
and now
there's nothing I can do.

Cancer took the one I loved,
and took a piece of me, too.

BLEEDING OUT

When someone dies,
you must understand
that a piece of you dies with them.
You're bleeding out,
clawing at thin air,
hoping you can live again.

You must get it through your head
that everything you once knew
is gone,
and whether you like it or not
we are made of those
who have built and broken us.

To live is pain,
to die is gain,
but only for those who are dead.
The rest are left
bleeding out.
The puzzle isn't complete without them.

To write is to ramble on about the things
we cannot comprehend,
to ponder life in all its greatness.
But how can life be great
if it leaves you feeling
worthless and hopeless?
I'm unfinished,
broken,
bleeding out.
Hurting in places no one can fix me.

Let Her Go

My heart's broken,
splintered into pieces.
Bits of me are lying everywhere.
The shock was over in minutes,
but the empty feeling remains.
My mind is trying to process what just happened.
Sick to the stomach,
I'm not okay.
I'm a whirlwind of emotions.
My heartbeat quickens,
I can't breathe.
What am I going to do?
I don't want to let her go.

Tidal Wave

The pain never goes away,
you just learn how to live with it.
It starts as a roaring tidal wave
and ends as a dull ache.

Isolated

To see her lying there,
weak,
vulnerable,
lonely
yet not alone,
reminds me too much
of myself.

Beauty Queen :,

Out of My Mind

Everything's blurry
and everything hurts.
This scares me,
and it's getting worse.
It's killing me,
I'm falling apart.
They say it's gonna get better
but they're lying to my heart.

RUNE

I'm empty,
there's nothing here.
I'm a hole
waiting to be filled.

Perthro, ⊠, the empty cup,
symbolizes something that's been hollowed out,
waiting to be filled again.
This is an accurate description of me.

NOTHING HAPPENED

Pretend that nothing happened.
If you can't see the problem,
is it really there?

Denial is your worst enemy
and your best friend.
Deny the facts,
believe the fiction.
Pretend nothing happened.

"No one forgets the truth; they just get better at lying."

—Richard Yates, *Revolutionary Road*

REALITY

What if she wants to believe the lies she tells herself
instead of the truth
she's being told?
What if she's not ready to face the world?

She hides her face in her hands
and with the mind of a child
believes it's going to get better.
But at some point
she has to face reality.

Goodbyes

"I'm dying," she whispered,
and when she looked at me
all the light I used to see,
all the joy,
all the love,
was gone.
There was only pain.
She wasn't happy.
She didn't want to go.
She didn't want to go,
yet she did.

TODAY

Today was the day I broke down.
Today was the day I realized
how big an impact she made.
The first person to ever show me love
has gone,
and taken all the joy with her.
Oh, cancer,
you are ruthless,
you are cruel.

> ## "I'm cold inside again, I'm an empty tunnel that meets a dead end."
>
> —Nova Ren Suma, *The Walls around Us*

It's today. This time last year, she left us. For good. And it still hurts. It's a numb kind of pain. A pain that you don't want to feel, but must. Humans are made to feel.

It's today. That's all I can say.

It's today.

Yesterday was fun. Tomorrow will be better. But not today.

One year ago today.

03/02/2018

It's stamped into my brain.

Today today today.

Maybe if I say it enough it'll lose meaning.

It's a numb kind of pain. I'm numb, and I'm in pain. Internal pain. Ghastly pain. All kinds of pain.

Ghosts, ghastly. Ghastly ghosts.

That's what they are.

Today.

SHE'S NOT HERE

Tell me why it hurts the way it does.
She's been gone for so long.
I should be healing,
back to feeling,
but the hole in my heart
just seems to get bigger.

And just when I think I'm getting better,
all the memories
slam into me
with the force
of a freight train.

Hopelessness
washes over me again.
It's a consuming darkness,
one that tells me
I'm worthless,
and she's not here
to piece me back together again.

To My Best Friend

"Sometimes me think, 'What is friend?'
Then me think, 'Friend is one to share last cookie with.'"

—Cookie Monster

When I Was a Burden

I've fallen so many times.
I've cried
on your shoulder.
You held me up
when I couldn't go on.
When I gave up
and sank into the deep,
you didn't leave me
drowning on my own.
You pulled me out
and helped me
back onto my feet.

You were my oxygen
when the world was pure poison,
you breathed life
into my
dead lungs.
You never gave up,
you never walked away,
even when I
was a burden.

Dear Best Friend,

I love you. I don't say it enough. You've been there through everything.

We're different, but at the same time so alike. I'm loud, you're quiet. I'm crazy, you're calm. I guess it's true that opposites attract. When I talk, you listen. And as you know, I talk. A lot.

We met in seventh grade, and we were friends from the beginning. Okay, maybe it took a little drama to bring us together, but once we found each other, it was like no one else mattered. We were ready to defend each other at a moment's notice.

And defend me you did. Seventh grade was bad. I'll admit it. But no matter how many times I came to lunch, or to PE, crying, you were always able to make me smile. You knew all the right things to say. You knew exactly which one of our hundreds of stupid inside jokes would make me laugh. You knew that all I needed was to be loved. All I needed was to know that somebody, anybody, cared.

You know my past. You know my insecurities and how people took advantage of them.

You know me inside out. Sometimes I think you know me better than I do.

There are times we go for weeks without speaking, but it has never damaged our friendship. When we get together, we pick up right where we left off. We fill each other in on all the petty drama. We rant and then we let it go. Once I talk to you, I'm good.

We've never needed anybody else because we have each other. At least, that's how I've always felt. Yes, I'll always have friends, but you've always been, and hopefully will always be, my number one. Everyone else falls beneath you.

So, thank you. Thank you for being there, for cheering me up, for being my moon in the darkness.

You take care of me, and I'd like to think that I've taken care of you.

I can't possibly put into words how much I love you.

Love,

Your derpy best fran,

Priscilla

NO PROB-LLAMA

That's So Random

"when things don't go right, go
left."

—Taco Bell Sauce Packet

"I try not to think. It interferes
with being nuts."

—Rick Riordan, Mark of Athena

Rain

I see raindrops
I see clouds
I see lightning
and I hear the thunder rumbling.

Some people want to dance in the rain
but I am quite content
to just
watch it
fall.

RAMBLINGS OF A MADMAN

This is why
this is why.
Please don't make me
regret that I tried.
Don't make me regret
all the good times
we've had.
Don't make me regret
all the smiles
we've shared.
I'm trying,
trying to reach out.
Falling,
falling into doubt.
I opened up,
I let you in.
Don't crush my heart
in the palm
of your hand.

Sanity,
insanity,
distinguished by a single
in.
Who decides
what's sane
and what's not?
Sanity isn't a choice.

It's an opinion.
We don't get to choose
of our own free will,
we don't get to decide
that we are stable,
chemically balanced,
call it what you will.
So beware
the ramblings
of the madman,
for he might not be
mad at all.

STAY
WEIRD

I'M SORRY
I'M LATE I
DIDN'T WANT
TO COME

NORMAL
PEOPLE
SCARE ME

NOT
TODAY
SATAN

JEALOUSY

Is it jealousy
if you're just trying
to protect
what was yours
to begin with?
They kill me,
these walls,
I can't get past them.
I feel like
a mime in a box
searching in vain
for an exit
that isn't there.
But I'm just
as bad as he,
seeing as how
I bury
all the things
I don't want to feel
deep down
inside of me.
I'm not one
to open up
and let people in
for fear
that eventually
they'll toss me aside
like I never meant
a thing to them.

Take Me Back

You're happy,
you're sad,
you've got that melancholy feeling in your heart.
You torture yourself with memories
but you can't do this to yourself forever.

They take you back,
back to times you wish had stayed.

The smell of the smoking fire
and marshmallows on a stick.
Happy seventh birthday,
happy tenth.
Bunk beds,
pools,
toes in the sand.
Frigid snow,
hot chocolate.
Performances,
recitals,
and spring programs.

"Take me back, take me back."
It's a plea that'll never be answered.
Those times are long gone.

"Take me back.
Take me back.
Please, God, take me back."

SOULMATES

I thought we were soulmates,
till she took you away.

Like Peter Pan,
she reached out her hand
and promised you Neverland
and together you flew away
without even saying
goodbye.

THE SHOWERHEAD

Water rains from the showerhead.
She closes her eyes
and lets it envelop her,
because she's hoping
that for once
she can drown in something
other than her thoughts.

"It was dark and cold and empty.
But there were stars. It was too
lonely to be heaven, and there
wouldn't be stars in hell."

—Kali Wallace, Shallow Graves

Revelations & Epiphanies

Between Reality and Fiction

I live on the border between reality
and fiction.
I'm here
and I'm not.
When I feel my world
falling apart,
I close my eyes
and picture the sky.
I imagine it crumbling into pieces,
then, reaching up to heaven,
I sew the broken pieces back together.

The glass of reality cracks under my feet,
threatening to give,
but I close my eyes
and imagine it breaking in reverse,
the broken pieces becoming oddly perfect
again.

I live on the border between reality and fiction.
I've learned that nothing is as it seems.

The chains of reality keep me anchored to this world. Fake fronts and masks have never worked on me. I see people for who they really are, not what they pretend to be. I know how cruel and unforgiving this world and its people can be. Pain and heartbreak are no strangers to me. And yet, I'm probably the biggest optimist you'll ever meet. I see people for who they are, but also, more importantly, for who they could be. I choose to believe that even the worst people have at least *some* good in them. I choose to believe that this world is better than it seems because if I didn't, I'd be one severely unhappy person. I prefer to keep my head in the clouds, where no one and nothing can hurt me. When life gets tough, I can retreat to that little space in my head and block out every thought and feeling and circumstance that isn't happy. And although I know that may not be healthy, this is how I've dealt with my problems my whole life. I block out the bad and focus on the good. I'm physically here, but my mind is always somewhere else.

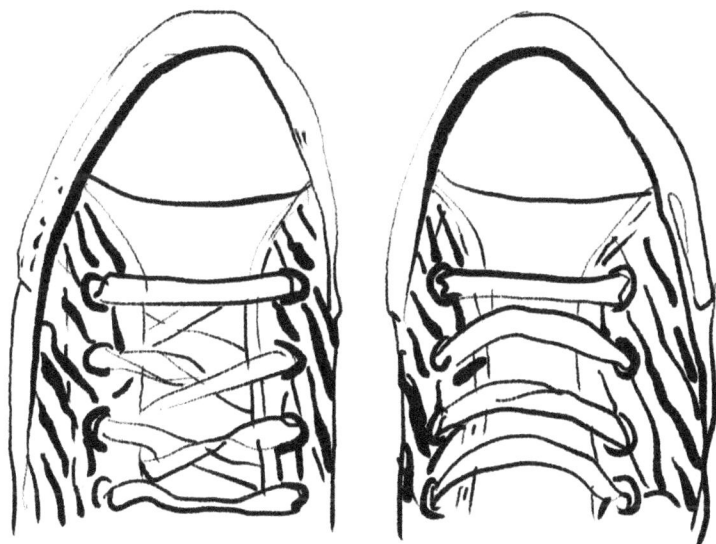

THINKING ABOUT IT

It's in my head.
Why can't I make it stop?

Thinking is good, yes,
but good things do turn bad

when you think about them
too much.

THE LAND OF CONCLUSIONS

I was right when I said one should never jump.
That wasteland is a terrible place to be.

Not all who wander are Lost ♡♡

Abnormal

You must understand
that I am not normal.
I'm about as far from normal
as a person can get.
I am abnormal,
and that's okay.

Be yourself

LONELY

You know you're lonely
when you talk to yourself,
when the only time you cry
is in the shower,
or at night,
when you have conversations with people
who aren't there.
It's exhausting, really,
having no one but yourself.

You know you're lonely when your chest feels empty,
your eyes heavy,
when all you want to do is go to bed,
knowing that sleep is your only reprieve,
the only time of the day
you're truly happy.

You know you're lonely
when the only way
for you to talk about your problems
is to write them down
with the hope that somehow
writing about it
will make you feel better.

"The worst part of being truly alone is you think about all the times you wished that everyone would just leave you be. Then they do, and you are left being, and you turn out to be terrible company."

—John Green, Turtles All the Way Down

LEAP OF FAITH

Take a leap of faith.
I know it's hard,
but you can do it.
Chin up,
don't slip.
Don't spill your soul to someone
who'll take one look
and walk away.

Open up,
do something you've never done.
Make friends,
find someone who cares.
Take that leap.

From Victim to Victor

"Even the darkest night will end/and the sun will rise."

—Herbert Kretzmer, Les Misérables (musical)

To the Woman Who Birthed Me, and to the Man Who Fathered Me

Thank you, Mother,
for not loving me,
thank you, Father,
for not wanting me enough
to choose me.
Because you chose drugs
over the children
you made,
you instilled in me
the desire
to make everyone around me happy.
Because of the pain
you put me through,
I came out a survivor,
able to smile when I don't want to,
to help people
who've been hurt, too.
Because of your neglect
I ended up
in a better place.

I was a victim
of your inconstant
love, attention,
and affection.

But I am a victim no more.
I haven't seen you
in over a decade.
I don't remember your faces,
don't remember your voices.
I grew up without you,
I don't need you.
I was a victim,
but not anymore.

I came out on top.
I am a victor,
a winner,
a daughter
with a mother and a father
who actually love her.

VICTIM TO VICTOR

I was a victim
of heinous crimes
so emotionally crippling
that I was left broken.
I was told that I'd never be enough
and that I wasn't worth the effort,
that the pain I was feeling
was God paying me back
for all the hurt I had caused.

They called me a monster
incapable of love.
They locked me in my room:
punishment
for my wrongdoings.
She had cold, dead eyes;
Satan reincarnate.
She took from me
everything I loved.

Little Care Bear,
small and yellow,
light of my life
and the only thing I had ever loved.
When she thought
I wasn't watching,
she took him
and threw him away
because he was a reminder
of the sad, hard life
her six-year-old
foster daughter
had already lived,

a reminder of the mother
she'd never be.
I hated her for that
for years and years.

The eleventh foster home
scarred me,
but I am not a victim
anymore.
I will not live in the past
and torture myself
with memories
of a life
I didn't want.
I will remind myself
of all the things I have.

I am no longer a victim,
I'm a victor.

I've won.

I am here,
and I am alive,
and I am breathing,
and I am happy.
I *am* enough,
I *can* love,
and I *am* loved.
I am not the monster
they made me out to be.
I will not let them
take from me
anymore.

They took my happiness
and they took my smile,
but they won't keep
their spoils of war.
I am here,
alive and well,
and I am taking back
what they unjustly
stole.

I am no longer a victim
but a victor.
They won't keep me locked up
anymore.

Epilogue:
The Past

LOOK BACK

People say never look back,
but if you never look back
how will you know if you're making
the same mistake twice?
I say
look back,
but keep walking forward.

The truth? I'm scared of my future. I'm terrified of what it may hold. It may hold good things, yes, but it's bound to hold bad things, too. I hate change, but change is inevitable, and it will come whether I want it or not.

For a long time I was so scared of the future that I was stuck in the past. I was so scared of moving forward that I was unknowingly holding myself captive. I wanted to fix what had been broken, to fix my heart. I was holding on to an old pain, cradling it gently as if it were some fragile being. I wanted to heal it, to keep it alive. But the harder I tried, the sicker it became. The wounds kept growing, getting wider and deeper.

I was scared of my ghosts and tired of being haunted. I was tired of being reminded of all the things I had failed to keep.

But I didn't want to let them go. Letting go felt like giving up, and I didn't want to give up all the people and things that had hurt me, even if they had already given up on me. It was a terrible dilemma.

Growing up in foster care, all I had were lies and broken promises. I had no real family, so when I finally got one, I assumed that they would be there forever. When I finally made friends, I assumed that they would stay forever, too. I never imagined that those friends would stab me in the back. I never imagined that they would cause me so much pain. So when they did betray me, I crawled back to them. I refused to believe, refused to let them go. I didn't cut them off when I should have. I naively believed that they still loved me, that they still cared.

Someone once said that holding a grudge is like drinking poison and expecting the other person to die instead. The grudge hurts the one who holds it, and meanwhile the person grudged is none the wiser. After all, they can't read your mind. So I finally realized that I had to let the grudges go. I didn't have a choice anymore. It was unhealthy. I was depressed and bitter. I was living in a world without color.

Then I did it. I stopped poisoning myself and let go of all the people who had driven knives into my back. I was finally able to stop living in the past and start living in the present. I was finally able to look ahead to my future. I was free.

> "There are things that have to be forgotten if you want to go on living."
>
> —Jim Thompson, *The Killer Inside Me*

People tell you to never look back, to leave your regrets and mistakes behind. "Forget"—they always say we should forget. I think that's wrong. If we don't look back, if we don't remember the mistakes we've made and all the decisions we regret, we might end up doing the same stupid thing over and over again. History repeats itself, but it doesn't have to. Not if we remember.

So I say, look back. Remember your mistakes. Let them remind you of who you used to be, of the person you no longer are. If you can remember, you can work on transforming yourself into the person you want to become. You can work on becoming someone better.

I look back, but I no longer dwell on my mistakes. I look and remind myself of the hateful person I used to be, and I smile, because I'm not that person anymore. I'm not bitter, and I'm not mad. I'm happy now, happier than I've ever been. Yes, I still have bad days, but now I am able to let the bad days go.

I'm happy. I have friends who love me, care for me, and understand me better than I ever could have imagined. I have an amazing family that puts up with me and supports me through everything. I have a future. I have plans for my last year in high school. I know what I want to do with my life: I want to write and teach children with special needs.

"It's no use going back to yesterday, because I was a different person then."

—Lewis Carroll, Alice's Adventures in Wonderland

So, when you look back, don't forget to keep walking forward. You can't start the next chapter of your life if you are still rereading the previous one.

www.ingramcontent.com/pod-product-compliance
Lightning Source LLC
Chambersburg PA
CBHW020257030426
42336CB00010B/805